know
the
game

Judo

by Geof Gleeson

Published by A & C Black (Publishers) Ltd
35 Bedford Row, London WC1R 4JH

Con

C000215464

The Author - Geof Gleeson

Many years member and captain of British judo teams. Captained the Champion European Team, Champion in European individual event. One-time Chief National Coach, creator of the national coaching scheme. Has lectured on and taught judo in many countries throughout the world. One-time European judo referee and member of the national executive committee of the British Judo Association. First foreign Special Research Student at the Kodokan, Japan. 7th dan judo and has trained in many of the martial arts whilst in Japan. Has written several major books on judo, and made an award-winning series of coaching films and several TV programmes. Has swum at national level and plays many sports. Founder member of the British Association of National Coaches. Holds Higher National Certificate of Engineering. Read Japanese at London University. D.M.S. (Rec.) London. Has lectured on sports hall management and sociology of leisure, and teaches Japanese. Has engaged in research for higher degree in sport sociology at the Polytechnic of North London. At present is Executive Secretary of the British Association of National Coaches.

Jigoro Kano (1860-1938)

Founder and creator of judo, or to give it its full name Kodokan Judo. He graduated from Tokyo University (the Oxbridge of Japan) in 1881, obtaining a master's degree in English and politics. While at university he trained in a couple of jujitsu schools. On graduation he was appointed lecturer at the most prestigious academy in Japan, the Peers School. In the same year he founded Kodokan Judo. Later Kano was made temporary principal of the Peers School. In 1889 he was sent to Europe to study Western educational methods and ideologies. (He was much impressed with the writings of J. S. Mill.) Upon his return to Japan he was appointed Principal of the Shihon Gakko, another very prestigious college, and made Council Member within the educational branch of the Civil Service. He was appointed Japanese representative on the International Olympic Committee and remained in that position till his death. Kano's very heavy commitment to the educational programme of the Japanese Government, where he held special responsibility for the physical education programme, tended to take him away from his part-time love, judo. However, naturally he maintained strong links with the developing sport and it was the prestige he contributed to it that was largely responsible for maintaining it through the Second World War and the period of American occupation. After that it began to pick up and develop momentum again. Thanks largely to the work of Britain and France, it gradually evolved into the international sport it is today. Undoubtedly Kano was a giant figure on the international landscape of physical education.

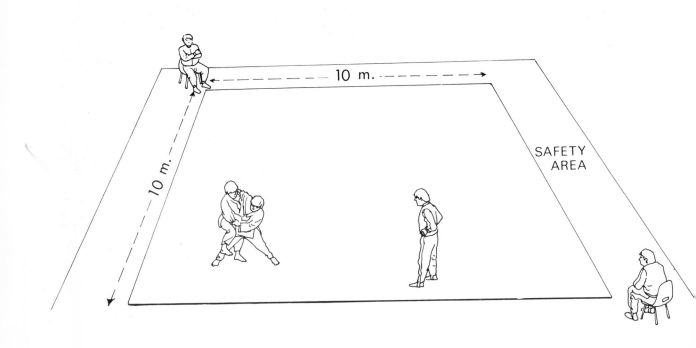

10 m.

10 m.

SAFETY AREA

Fig. 1 Contest area

Introduction

Fig. 2

Judo in the 'wide sense' can be physical culture; in the 'narrow sense', a sport. As physical culture it can be an entrance into a special form of physical experience – an expression of an intrinsic need, an increase of awareness of what the body is capable of doing. As a sport the individual can participate in aggressive competition, experience the conflict of one skill opposed to another. As a man-made skill it can develop the bad as well as the good in any personality; a critical factor in deciding which way to go is the coach or teacher.

Judo is a style of wrestling; the participants wear special clothing (see fig. 2), which facilitates the performance of the many skills involved. Judo originated in Japan about a hundred years ago, and has been practised in Britain for about sixty years. Judo, because it is wrestling, is potentially dangerous, therefore every precaution must be taken to minimise the risks. There must be a mat, which should be at least 8m square if more than four people are doing judo simultaneously (10m in competition – see fig. 1). It must be thick enough to absorb the momentum of a falling body weight. The mat surface should be free from folds and wrinkles, or any other obstacles that could trap and hence injure the feet. There must be no gaps in the mat area, allowing parts or even the whole body to strike the hard floor under the mats. If a group, e.g. over four, is learning the skills simultaneously, they must be made aware that the other people on the mat (not just their partner) can be a potential hazard. They must develop a 'radar' sense of where other people are and how to avoid them as they move around. No-one should lie down aimlessly on the mat, so providing an object for others to trip over. When not actually participating, people should stand round the mat watching – and learning from – the others. In short, judo is a *group* activity and a group feeling of safety and co-operation must be cultivated.

Judo is traditionally done in bare feet (see fig. 2), and therefore hygiene is important. Some form of foot covering must be worn between mat and changing area. Whenever the mat is left the foot covering should be worn. It goes without saying that the feet themselves must be clean and well looked after.

The special judo suits can be bought from most sports shops. They are made very strongly, so that they can withstand the enormous amount of pulling and pushing that goes on during free play. They are all-white, as in the photograph on this page. The black trousers shown elsewhere in the book are used for clarification of the illustrations.

6

A throw by experienced players

The Skills

In such a small book as this only a 'taster' can be offered, but indeed that is the object of this series. When the time comes for you to want more information about judo you will find a much deeper and more detailed coverage in *All About Judo* (EP Sport series).

In brief, there are two general skills to be learnt in judo; a tactical skill and a technical skill. The technical skill comprises those precise movements which, when added together, either throw your partner to the ground or make him submit, as a result of various grappling movements. The tactical skill is the creation of the right circumstances in which a technical skill can be performed, or the linking together of several technical skills in order to bring about a predetermined end. Such an 'end' can be a winning throw, or it can mean the production of a situation in which the opponent is unable to make an attack – a good achievement in a competitive sport! From such definitions you can see that the tactical skill is in many ways more important than the technical one – but that does not mean the technical skills can be treated lightly. It is hoped that this book will introduce you to both.

How to Start

First read the whole of this book two or three times if you can, so that you have an overall picture of what judo is all about. Find yourself a partner, or better still get together with several friends who want to learn. The more the better, for then you can swap ideas and methods. You can start almost anywhere, either by learning a throwing technique or a grappling one; some people – especially if they are particularly athletic – will prefer to begin with the tactical skills. The average age of the group is what normally decides a coach where to start: if the learners are young he will start with a throwing technique, if not so young a grappling technique. The orthodox method is to begin with a throwing technique. Start by putting yourself into the position shown in fig. 2. See where you will be holding, how your bodies relate one to another, but before you actually try it on the mat, find out how you will get from the standing (vertical) position to the lying down (horizontal) position.

Change of Dimension

Look carefully at fig. 3a–e. Stand on both feet (3a); step forward with right foot and half turn (3b). Stand on right foot – pivot – sit down, facing where you have come from

Fig. 3a

Fig. 3b

Fig. 3c

8

(3c). Keeping your arms and head tucked in, roll back (3d and e). Try it several times till you can do it easily with little thinking, and no bangs or bumps as you get down to the floor. Here is the first way of learning how to 'fall' down. There are many others.

Technical Throwing Skill No. 1 (Legs Astride Throw)

So now take up the position as in fig. 2. Look at fig. 4a as well. See how and where your hands should be gripping – compare figs. 2 and 4a. What about feet? Do your feet match those of the men in fig. 4a? This is the starting position for all throwing skills, so it is important to get it right. Indeed fig. 4a will be the starting position for every throwing technique's explanation – it will always be fig. Xa; for example, fig. 6a is omitted because it is the same as fig. 4a. Good! Let's start. Now, make a short step forward with your right foot; using that foot as a pivot, take the left foot back, behind the right foot – it should have the effect of half turning your body. Now put the right foot out (4b), letting the body turn completely.

Fig. 3d

Fig. 3e

Repeat several times with your partner just standing still: right foot, left foot, right foot; the pattern and rhythm are important. When you are comfortable with it, do it once more, but now when your legs are astride, let the partner step over the outstretched leg (fig. 4c). The partner then pivots, sits and rolls, as he did in fig. 3c–e (see fig. 4d).

Fig. 4a

Fig. 4c

Caution

To describe a throw in its very simplest terms is to say put an arm, a leg or a part of your body in front of (or behind) your partner and *push* him over it. So in a legs astride throw, the attacker's right leg is put across the legs of the partner and he is *pushed* over it. See how in fig. 4b the attacker is pushing the partner forward with his right hand.

The partner should begin to step over that right leg *before* it is in position, thus ensuring it is *he* who takes the initiative in 'falling down'. During these early days of learning and training there is no competition, only co-operation.

Fig. 4d

A Tactical Skill

Judo is a tactical competition. There is much movement and therefore techniques must be performed – and learnt – during movement. Trying to throw while moving in any direction can be confusing, so let us try to use fig. 5 to make it clear. Let the attacker push the partner towards white back; the partner responds by walking naturally backwards; the attacker follows. After two or three steps he attacks as when they were standing still – right foot, left foot, right foot – trying to push/throw the partner into the quadrant black side/black front, but now he must take into account the different spaces created by the movement. The partner steps over just as before, sits and rolls over. Try it several times. Change roles.

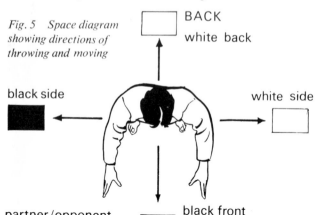

Fig. 5   *Space diagram showing directions of throwing and moving*

BACK
white back

black side

white side

black front
FORWARD

12   partner/opponent

Technical Throwing Skill No. 2 (Inside-Leg Block)

Fig. 6b

Start as in fig. 4a, move the feet as at the beginning of the legs astride throw – right foot, left foot – now hook right leg in behind the partner's left leg (6b). Push him in the quadrant white back/black side (6c).

Caution
Partner skips right foot back, clears his left leg from the attacker's hooking leg, and sits and rolls backwards (6d).

A Tactical Skill
It is in these backward throwing techniques where something, i.e. a leg, is placed *behind* the partner and he is pushed over that. Now the attacker pulls his partner *forward* – towards the black front. After a few steps the technique is attempted. The partner ensures he keeps his legs apart, to facilitate the attack – remember it is co-operation now, not competition.

Fig. 6c

Fig. 6d

13

Technical Grappling Skill No. 1 (Side-Body Pin)

Just as a throwing technique must be learnt in movement, in order to ensure it will quickly become a tactical skill, so grappling skills too must be learnt during movement. Many different situations could be devised in which such skills could be learnt and no doubt as you get better you will produce your own situations. However, here a defensive position will be used as the start. A defensive position is with the partner on his elbows and knees (in this position, with experience, he would be able to block most attacks). The attacker, from the side, slips his hands under the partner and clasps his hands round his right elbow (fig. 7a). By pulling the elbow and pushing with the chest (see how the attacker's legs are pushing, 7b), the attacker turns the partner over (7b) and finishes in the side-body pin position (7c).

Notice where the attacker's left hand is, see how the

Fig. 7a

Fig. 7b

weight is bearing down on the shoulders and chest of the partner 'pinning' him to the ground. The attacker's right hand is holding the trousers of the partner, so controlling the movement of his legs.

In competition, to hold an opponent this way for 30 seconds would score a 'terminal 10', that is, an immediate, winning finish. Less than 30 seconds – 25 or 20 or 15 seconds – would score respectively 7, 5, or 3.

Caution

To be on the back is a losing position. To be thrown on the back loses a 'terminal 10', so it is good training never to allow the back to touch the ground. Always practise staying off it, lying on the side, sitting, anything but the back. Get to feel uncomfortable if you ever find yourself on your back.

A Pin Break-Out

Not easy of course! Even when done by a skilful player it takes a great deal of effort to break free from a pin.

Fig. 8a

Fig. 7c

Fig. 8b

15

However, the foundation of any break-out is the 'bridge' (see fig. 8). Practise on your own. Lie down as in fig. 8a. Have your hands ready to 'push' off the opponent. Lift the hips up into the 'bridge' (8b). Now turn strongly and quickly one way, 'pushing' off the opponent. Again, and turn the other way.

When under a pin, the bridging is to make space between the bodies, in order to get the hands in a position to push. Once ready to push, the body 'bridges' again, but turns also – hopefully thrusting off the attacker. It is not easy. It needs practice.

Fig. 9b

Technical Throwing Skills
Nos. 3, 4 and 5

By modifying slightly the inside-leg block, three more throws can easily be learnt.

No. 3 Outside-Leg Block
The attack starts the same as before (fig. 4a), right foot

then left foot, but now the attacker's right leg instead of going inside goes on the outside of the partner's right leg (9b). Push in the quadrant white back/black side (see fig. 5).

No. 4 Inside-Leg Stop
The right foot first moves as before, but now the left foot

Fig. 9d

Fig. 9e 17

moves towards the partner's right foot (see fig. 9c). The push of the attacker is in the quadrant white back/white side (fig. 5).

No. 5 Outside-Leg Stop
The right foot moves as before, left foot to near partner's right foot (see fig. 9d). The leaning body-weight of the attacker pushes the partner into the quadrant white back/white side.

Caution
As with the inside-leg block the partner in all three throws (figs. 9b–d) hops back on the leg he is standing on, clears the other leg and sits and rolls back (9e). Try to keep the attack and the sit-down as smooth and bumpless as possible. It should all be 'easy'.

A Tactical Skill
As before, with any of these back-throws the attacker starts by pulling the partner *forwards* – towards black front (see fig. 5). After a few steps, one of the attacks can be tried. Which one? As frequently happens, it may be the partner (opponent) who sets up the opportunity – has he got his legs apart or together? If together, the 'outside' throws; if apart the 'inside' throws; if he moves quickly the 'stop' throws; if he moves slowly the 'block' throws.

Fig. 10a

18

More Ways of Getting Down to the Ground

Eventually, when the competitive element is introduced into training (but not yet though), throwing becomes more severe. Each competitor naturally tries to stop the other from throwing him, so when he is finally thrown, the fall can be a heavy one. Various ways of falling can be learnt to minimise the impact of such falls. The reader can now begin to learn some of the fundamentals of these falling ways in readiness for the future.

It has already been shown that if a throw is made sideways and the fall is sideways, a foot and then the bottom can be used as the initial shock-absorber. Certainly such falls will be found in championship judo. But sometimes the fall is straight forward, over the throwing attacker. What to do then?

Let one person get down on hands and knees (and make himself 'strong'). The other man stands at the side, holds – with both hands – the nearest side of the jacket (fig. 10a); he rolls over, keeping his head tucked under, and *off the ground*. During the movement through space, the man makes sure his feet get in front of the movement, so hitting the ground first (10c). The important points here are that the head is kept clear of the ground and the feet

Fig. 10d

19

hit first, absorbing much of the impact.

Sometimes the legs cannot be used this way, and the shock-absorbing must be done by an arm. Start the same way (10a and b), but now when half way over free one of the arms – in this instance the right arm (10d) – and just before the body hits the ground, hit the ground with the whole length of the right arm. Again it is keeping the head off the ground which is important.

With practice, and in practice, these seemingly different ways can be mixed up, and whichever part is more important – feet, bottom. arms – can be made dominant. The situation will dictate the type of fall to be used, so not only must the good judo performer be able to do all types of falling but must be flexible enough in attitude to use the appropriate one at an instant's notice.

Caution

If at any time head-over-heels actions are performed (for whatever reason) remember to keep the head off the ground. That is the object of falling – to save the head and allow the body to absorb the impact in the safest way possible. In any case, solo falling skills have very little relevance to a throwing situation, as they lack that essential ingredient, the other person. It is the 'other person' who forces the fall, and that is the factor that must be built into any training method of falling.

Technical Throwing Skill No. 6
(One-Arm Shoulder Throw)

Fig. 11b

Start as fig. 4a. The attacker steps forward with the right foot, freeing the grip of his right hand; his left foot swings back – between the partner's feet (see fig. 11b). He then kneels on right knee. Notice carefully the relative position of the attacker to the partner in fig. 11b. By simply tucking forward, the attacker rolls the partner over his shoulders (11c). The direction is straight at black front (see fig. 5).

Caution

The partner can use any of the ways of 'falling' he has learnt so far: step-round, sit, roll; head over heels, roll forward; roll forward, using feet as shock-absorbers; roll forward, using beating arm as shock-absorber. Benefit will be gained from all.

A Tactical Skill

Keep to the usual pattern for a start – the attacker pushes his partner back, towards white back (see fig. 5). After a few steps, step in, turn, drop to the knee and roll the partner over. Forward and backward movements are not of course the only directions the performers can move in, so let's try a new one. The partner moves in a circle towards white side. The attacker tries as before, but now he must make allowances for the circular movement of the partner. You will no doubt find that a considerable amount of modification will be needed in the turn into the throwing action of fig. 11c.

Fig. 11c

Technical Grappling Skill No. 2 (Straight-Arm Lock)

There are three forms of grappling skills that can be used for scoring points in competition. The pinning techniques have already been mentioned; the other two are the arm-locks and strangles, the object here being to inflict pain so that the opponent submits, which loses him 10 points and the match. Let us now look at one of these arm-locks.

As with the pinning techniques, the arm-locks must be learnt in a tactical situation. The partner gets on his knees and elbows (fig. 12a); the attacker holds the sleeve and the belt (the belt-hold is to help to control the movement of the partner); quickly he moves his left foot up, stands on it and pivots into the astraddle position (12b), holding tightly the partner's right arm. The attacker falls back into the position shown in fig. 12c. By straightening out the right arm and 'bending it' over the right thigh, a 'lock' is put on the elbow joint.

Caution

Great care must be taken when these techniques are being learnt, as lasting damage can be done if the locks are applied too enthusiastically. The partner must always tap

his submission long before any actual pain is felt.

Also when training the attacker should keep the grip *on the elbow at all times*. In this way risk of injury is kept to a minimum. Only in competition should the grip be changed to the *wrist*, so that pain can be inflicted.

Fig. 12c

A Tactical Skill

Straight-arm locks can be applied in many situations. It is beneficial to 'invent' your own particular best time of application.

Look for the time when he pushes you with a straight arm; does he try and keep you 'at arm's length' with a straight arm? These are all good opportunities.

 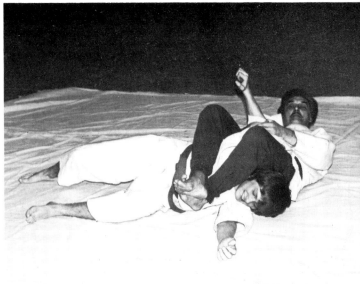

Fig. 12b   Fig. 12c

Technical Grappling Skill No. 3 (One-Hand Strangle)

Again, start with the partner on his elbows and knees (fig. 13a). The attacker slips his left hand under the neck and holds the right collar as deep as possible. He quickly straddles the partner, slipping his feet into the partner's thighs, and tucks his right hand under the right arm of the partner (13b). By using the legs and his arms, the attacker rolls the partner over, and thrusts his right arm behind the partner's head (13c). To apply the strangle, the left hand pulls hard across the throat (holding tight to the collar), while the right arm pushes the head forward onto the 'cutting' left wrist (13d).

Caution
To reiterate, these strangling techniques can be dangerous and should be learnt with care. The partner must tap his submission long before the strangle is really effective.

Fig. 13a

Fig. 13b

A Tactical Skill

The first thing is that the attacker must be able to attack from both sides of the partner. When you try doing it on the other side remember it is the right hand that goes across the neck first. All the rest changes accordingly.

Let us now try it as a 'follow-up' to a throw. Attack with one of the backward throws (to white back). The partner skips out, sits down, rolls right over – onto his elbows and knees. Now can the attacker follow him down and apply the strangle you have just learnt? You may not be able to choose which side you attack from: would the arm-lock be easier? Perhaps now you can begin to see the excitement of wrestling skills!

Fig. 13c Fig. 13d

Technical Throwing Skill No. 7
(Blocking-Foot Throw)

There are many throws in judo which incorporate the principle of tripping an opponent. One way is to knock his foot out from under him, as he is about to put his weight on it, while the other stops his foot from moving and he is forced to fall over it. Most of these techniques, because of the subtlety of timing, are very difficult to do; the one given here is one of the easier ones.

Starting as fig. 4a, the attacker steps forward with his left foot, if possible past the partner's right foot (fig. 14b). He places his right foot on the left instep of the partner (14b). Using his whole body-weight he then pushes the partner over that trapped foot into the quadrant white side/black front (see fig. 5).

Caution
The partner steps over the blocked foot with his left foot, pivots, sits and rolls, as he has done before, only now it is the opposite way. It means of course that the movement shown in fig. 3 should be practised both ways.

A Tactical Skill
This is a very useful tactical throw because it can be linked

Fig. 14b

with so many others, either to prepare the opponent for a subsequent terminal attack or to finish a whole series of attacks, the objective of which is to unstabilise the opponent. For example, if the blocking foot is tried, the opponent will frequently step over it (just as has happened at this very elementary level). As he moves away the attacker will quickly follow him and attack again with the legs astride throw.

An alternative! The attacker moves in and attempts an inside-leg block, the opponent lifts the blocked leg high (again just as has happened at the elementary level) and takes several steps backwards; again the attacker quickly follows him and attacks again with the blocking-foot throw.

Even with the few throws the reader has at his/her disposal at the moment, the blocking-foot throw could be linked in many ways with them, to build up a good repertoire. Let the reader try.

Technical Grappling Skill No. 4 (Diagonal Pin)

Look at fig. 15. Look at it carefully, try and replicate it. Check points: weight on right hip and right elbow, so bridging the opponent and pinning his chest to the ground; legs wide astride, acting as stabilisers to prevent turning; feet on the ground facilitating fast and strong movement, which is necessary to counter the moves of the partner when trying his break-out.

Caution

The partner will be trying to out-manoeuvre the attacker, moving one way then quickly reversing and going the other way. The attacker has got to try and retain the original body-relationship (fig. 15), so he must move as quickly and as much as the partner – only not enough to get himself in an unstable position, where the partner can easily tip him over.

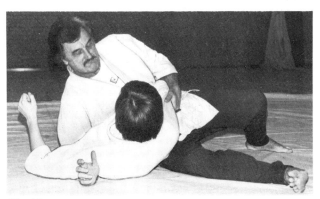

Fig. 15

A Tactical Skill

Let the attacker try the legs-astride throw. The partner steps over, sits and rolls; the attacker moves forward (having let go) and waits for an opportunity to quickly nip in and secure the diagonal pin. As before, with the strangle, make sure you can do the pin with equal facility from the other side of the partner; in the 'heat of battle' you will not have much time to decide from which direction you attack.

Technical Throwing Skill No. 8 (Inside-Leg Lift)

The first two steps of the attacker are the same as before: right foot, left foot; the attacker's left foot *outside* of partner's left foot (16b). The right leg swings back and up, lifting the partner's left leg high (16c). The attacker, using his body-weight, pushes into the quadrant black side/

Fig. 16b

black front, pulling the partner's head and shoulders down and round. The lift of the left leg and the push will roll the partner down.

Caution

Again the partner steps forward with his right foot and sits (16d) – and then rolls back (16e). The stepping out of the attack should be done before the left leg is raised very high.

A Tactical Skill

Notice how most of the initial attacking steps are the same; not only is this for ease of performance, but also to confuse the opposition – he has to guess which throw it will be. The experienced player will, in fact, make the opening moves intentionally as identical as possible, in order to camouflage his final action.

Similarly with the direction of attack. Start by pushing the partner backwards, towards white back. After a few

Fig. 16d   Fig. 16e

steps, step forward and swing the leg back and up (16c). But having done that, ask the partner to move in a circle, as in the one-arm shoulder throw, and try it then. Now ask him to move forwards. Try it again. Can you feel how the space between the bodies is affected by the direction of movement of the partner, and therefore how you will need to vary the range of turning to make the throwing action?

Again, try joining this throw 'in front of' and 'behind' other throwing techniques to make an attacking sequence. Remember the object of linking a series of attacking actions is to tire and confuse the opponent so that the final attack is both easier and more effective. To attack with just one technique, when the opponent is moving defensively and cautiously, is to give him too big an opportunity to negate the attack and seize the initiative.

Technical Grappling Skills Nos. 5 and 6 (Bent-Arm Locks)

The straight-arm lock has already been shown in fig. 12. For the bent-arm lock let the starting position be different (fig. 17a). Imagine the partner has been thrown, but not for a terminal score of 10, only 5 or 7. The attacker quickly moves in to try some grappling technique. (He may not even know what at this stage.) The partner

Fig

carelessly tries to push him off with his left arm (17a); the attacker sees the opportunity. His left hand moves and holds the partner's left wrist, the right hand goes under the left arm (17b). He holds on to his own left wrist and pushes the arm down to the ground (17c). By holding the wrist to the ground and raising the (partner's) elbow by lifting his own right elbow, the attacker causes pain – the lock – to the elbow.

Fig. 17b

Fig. 17c

Caution

Again, because of the potential danger of this lock, care must be used when learning how to apply it. Lift the elbow slowly and stop as soon as the partner makes *any* sign of pain or submitting. Joints, like the people they belong to, are all different. Some have a very wide range of flexibility, others have an extremely narrow one. What causes pain to one person may not to another. One person may have a lot of angular movement, another may not. These differences will need to be explored when learning how to apply arm-locks.

A Tactical Skill

The opportunity shown here is only one of many that suit a bent-arm lock. For example when using a diagonal pin (fig. 15), there are several opportunities generally offered for both arms. If the partner puts his left arm in front of the attacker's body to push him off, the attacker rolls forward into the lock; if the partner frees his right arm and pushes the attacker on the chest, there is another opportunity. See if you can work out precisely how they are done. You will need to use your imagination, but that is good for you – and judo.

Bent-Arm Lock No. 6

Let's go back to the defensive kneeling position for the start – fig. 18a. The attacker starts by holding the partner's left wrist with his right hand (18a). The attacker's left hand goes over and then under the partner's left arm to catch his own right wrist. The partner's left arm is then quickly lifted and the attacker

moves round fast to the side of the partner – see how the feet are ready to push or drive forward (18b). The partner is then pushed or turned over onto his back (18c); the attacker's weight is used to keep the partner down. The left hand (of the partner) is held on the ground, whilst the upper arm is lifted by the raising of the attacker's left elbow. Pain will be felt in the elbow and the shoulder.

Caution

The rules of judo competition specify that locks (pain) can be applied only to the elbow joint. Unfortunately, with this arm-lock it is impossible to isolate the twisting of the elbow from that of the shoulder joint. Judo does not appear to know that and referees continue to ignore the infringement. So do not worry that pain is felt at the shoulder – the referees will not – just be careful not to be too violent when doing it.

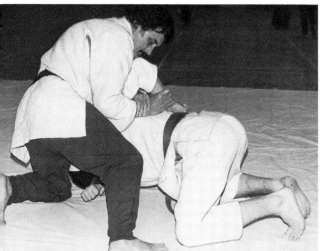

Fig. 18b   *Fig. 18c*

A Tactical Skill

Arm-locks of any kind are of a snatched, fleeting nature. They tend to produce an unstable position on the part of the attacker. In addition many competitors (but not all) do not like the possibility that they may sometimes *have* to inflict serious pain on the opponent, if he will not submit (as perhaps he may not, if there is a big championship at stake). Therefore arm-locks are not frequently used. However, for tactical training again, situations should be devised by the trainees (or their coach) to show how they can be applied.

Conclusion

It has already been said above that so far the learning of the skills displayed here has been an exercise in co-operation. Everyone involved has been trying to help everyone else, as well as to improve his own ability. The coach (and hopefully there has been one) has been helping with this process, not only encouraging each individual to apply himself fully, but getting the group to work together for the benefit of all.

When all have acquired more facility in performing the fourteen techniques and linking them together in various tactical combinations, perhaps it would be time to introduce the element of competition. Again if you want more information on this subject before you embark on it, it may be of benefit to read *All About Judo*. In the normal development of judo skills, movement plus competition is called 'free play' and it entails couples moving freely around the mat area, each person trying to score with the techniques and tactics he or she has learnt. When first experiencing free play, the apprehension of being thrown, as well as being thrown in spite of the attempts not to be, will tend to produce a very rigid, defensive, ponderous movement. Well, indulge yourself for a little while – but realise how negative the whole thing becomes if you do this.

Certainly the opponent will have great difficulty in throwing you, but then you will have just as much difficulty in throwing him. The object of free play is to improve the skills, and you will only achieve this if you use them. So you will need to stand up straight and get closer to the opponent, so that you can launch your attacks quickly and effectively. Competition of any kind has a large gambling element in it. Risks have to be taken. Risks that may go wrong and mean losing, or may go right and mean winning. In free play, for example, it is a risk to stand straight and move around easily, as your opponent may indeed throw you; but at the same time it is the only way to learn how to throw him!

After some experience of free play has been acquired, in which participants have gained some 'know-how' of dealing with very fluid situations and have discovered something about how to keep their wits about them under the stress of 'surviving', perhaps contests could be tried. Here the situation is more formal. There will be judges and referees. The rules of contest must be adhered to (which means they must be thoroughly known by the contestants). The matter of winning and losing takes on a more important role, yet not so important that it means the ethical principles of fair play and justice to the participants can be forgotten or ignored. Remember it is important to win *before* the match; it is not important *after* the match. Certainly the coach will advise on practical ways of fighting fair and giving sporting consideration to the opposition. Having got this far you will be quite capable of deciding for yourself which of the two judo objectives you wish to pursue. These objectives were simply defined by Jigoro Kano (the man who 'invented' judo), as being judo in the 'narrow sense', where skills acquired are used only in competitive sport; or judo in the 'wide sense', where the skills can be enjoyed for their own sake; where the lessons you learn on the judo mat – co-operation with your fellow participants, to give and receive justice, to fight hard but fair – can extend beyond the judo mat. Of course both forms of judo can be learnt at the same time, and should be. To attempt to pursue one at the cost of the other can only produce crudity of performance, degeneracy of spirit and vandalisation of the community.

National Judo Organisation

To reiterate: judo is a group activity. It cannot be done by oneself or even with a friend. To develop correctly there must be a range of opposition to 'sharpen' the skills upon. So you will need to join a club, and having considered clubs, the national organisation that services most of them should be looked at. There are several national judo organisations, each one offering its membership something slightly different from the others. The British Judo Association is one affiliated to the Central Council of Physical Recreation and represents the U.K. at the Olympic Games.

The various organisations have regional as well as national offices and from these centres information can be acquired about location of clubs and the general range of costs. In addition, information can be gathered from the various levels of the Sports Council, national, regional and local. However, not all clubs are affiliated to national associations. Some wish to remain independent and go their own way.

Efficiency and effectiveness of both teaching and administration is not the monopoly of any one judo organisation. Each club must be assessed on its own merit. For the newly enthusiastic – how should he or she judge? It is difficult to suggest exactly what points to look out for, but let me try to give some idea of the more obvious ones:

1. Are the mat and its environs clean; are the judo suits of the trainees clean? If dirty there is no way of telling how far the 'dirt' extends – into the coaching, into the organisation?

2. Is there a system of teaching, or are the members simply allowed to do perpetual free play? If so, progress is going to be very slow, very painful and very expensive.

3. Is there a special programme for the novice, or is he 'thrown in' among all the other members? If he is, again progress will be slow, painful and expensive.

4. Is there a feeling of group-awareness? Or is it every man and woman for themselves? If it is the latter and if you contemplate joining, make sure you are a 'loner'. It can get very lonely when you are left in the middle of a judo mat to look after yourself.

5. How are the contests arranged and why? Contests are usually fought under the rules of the International Judo Federation. National organisations distribute

copies and all clubs should have copies easily available. Occasionally contests are used to exploit the novice (the novice has to pay entrance fees). Try to ensure that contests are for your benefit, and not for the organisation.

If joining a club seems to be too big a step to start with, a good alternative is to try joining an introductory course organised by the Sports Council in conjunction with a governing body.

Judo Grades

All judo organisations have a 'grading system'. It purports to be an escalating series of tests, increasing in severity, which indicates an individual's standard of improving skill. There are two main groups that have to be 'climbed' through: the first set is named 'kyu' (pronounced 'Q'), the second 'dan'. In the early days of judo these two sets represented status within the total group. Nowadays such a social distinction no longer exists. The kyu grades are represented by different-coloured belts (usually going from the lighter colours to the darker), whilst the dan grades' belts are mostly black. There is a special class named 'mon' for the under-sixteens. The 'grading' concept originated in Japan, but now the systems have little practical similarity with the Japanese version.

Judo Contests

Enough has been said already to give a general idea of what is a contest, but a few more points may help. The duration of a match depends largely on the status of the match. A 'local' match can last as little as three minutes, whilst a major event – like the Olympics – can last fifteen minutes. There are no 'rounds' as in boxing. A 10-point scoring technique terminates a match immediately, victory going to the scorer. Scores of 3, 5, or 7 can be gained by part-throws or part-pins and then the best score at the end of time decides the winner. All nationally organised matches are weight-classified (much like boxing). However, it has not always been so. In my early days of competition there were no weight classifications: I frequently fought men 50–100 lb heavier than I was. Duration varied as well: I once fought the longest match ever – thirty minutes – in the European Championships. Lastly, but by no means least, the actual contest area varies considerably, but the international size is 10 m × 10 m.

Participation

As in most sports, all ages and both sexes can take part in judo. However, the skills will undergo considerable variations and changes to suit the widely differing types of participant. Judo skills depend largely upon power and speed, therefore the type of skill used by, for example, the Olympic competitor, will differ considerably from that of the person who is doing it 'just for fun'. That is why men and women do not have matches against each other and why even in training care must be taken if men are to train with women. Children too, particularly below the age of puberty, experience difficulty in learning the skills because the skills entail the control of two body-weights (their own and their partner's) and their immaturity, both physical and psychological, makes that difficult. However, to offset that they will get enormous pleasure from the body-contact of the wrestling.

For the young man judo offers the challenge of survival. Is he strong enough to overcome the forces that are trying to eliminate him from the competitive field? For the older man it can be an experience in co-operative movement; each one eliciting from the other the best skilled movements, by creating testing situations. For women, in addition to the above, it can offer a means of physical expression that is denied them in most other forms of competition. Because judo is oriental it has acquired the reputation of being non-violent, and society 'allows' women to participate in judo without accusing them of being masculine.

Terminology

Because judo is from Japan its terminology is Japanese. Many coaches and most text-books use Japanese words to label techniques and certain fundamental principles. Usually it is done for convenience. Every judo player is supposed to learn Japanese terminology. Sometimes it is used as a curtain to hide ignorance. (It is easier to humbug in Japanese than in English.) In case the reader would like to compare the techniques in this book with other books the following 'translations' are offered.

English	Equivalent Japanese
Legs astride (throw)	Tai-otoshi
Inside-leg block (throw)	Ouchi-gake
Side-body pin	Yoko-shiho-gatame
Outside-leg block (throw)	Osoto-gake
Inside-leg stop (throw)	Kouchi-gake
Outside-leg stop (throw)	Kosoto-gake
One-arm shoulder throw	Ippon-seoi-nage
Straight-arm lock	Ude-gatame
One-hand strangle	Kata-ha-jime
Blocking-foot (throw)	Sasai-tsurikomi-ashi
Diagonal pin	Kesa-gatame
Inside-leg lift (throw)	Uchi-mata
Bent-arm lock	Ude-garami
Methods of falling down	Ukemi
Free play	Randori
Competition	Shiai
Contest	Shobu

Index

Printed by Swannack, Brown & Co. Ltd., Hull, England.